Written by Kenneth Perry

Edited by Tiffany N. O'Brien

Photographs by Kenneth Perry, unless otherwise credited.

ISBN-10: - 1-946490-16-4

ISBN-13: - 978-1-946490-16-2

DEDICATION

I would like to dedicate this collection of planning guides to two influential people in my life, Joe, and Cindy Perry. My son, Joe Perry, for revitalizing me with the desire to search out and enjoy the beautiful country and its natural resources we have and to explore all of the National Parks; and my lovely wife, Cindy Perry, who supported me in the writing of this planning guide. I am very fortunate to find a unique woman that not only enjoys nature, travel, etc. but is always up for the next adventure.

ABOUT THE AUTHOR

Kenneth is a Certified Interpretive Guide (CIG) through the National Association of Interpretation (NAI) and has visited all of the 50 United States in addition to many European countries, the Caribbean, Mexico, and Canada. Kenneth has visited 31 National Parks and 34 National Monuments. Cindy has visited 33 National Parks, most of which were before their marriage, and are now going to see them together (Ahhh!). As of 2017, there are 59 National Parks and 84 National Monuments. They will be traveling in their motorhome to visit most of the parks, excluding Hawaii and the Virgin Islands. Bailey, their dog, has also been quite the little traveler.

Kenneth started providing trip planning in 2015 to aid travelers in getting the most out of their vacation. The books leverage off of in-depth field experience at each of the National Parks and Monuments. So whether you only have a day, week, or month, you will be provided with the must see and do activities.

The purpose of this planning guide is to provide you with a plethora (always loved that word from the movie "Three Amigos") of information before and during your trip so that you can focus on what you would like to spend your time on during your vacation. If you purchased the paperback, you could also download the eBook either for free or at a very minimal cost.

There are additional pictures posted on the website at NationalParkPlanningGuides.com for each of the parks that did not make it into my books. Feel free to copy and print them, or add them to your vacation slideshow/photos.

National Park Planning Guides Contact Information:

Website: NationalParkPlanningGuides.com
Facebook: www.facebook.com/NationalParkPlanningGuides/
Email: NationalParkPlanningGuidesInfo@gmail.com.

HOW TO USE THE PLANNING GUIDE

No matter whether you purchase the ebook or paperback, it will be a great planning resource to bring along on your trip to the national park. However, for some of the larger and more visited parks, I would suggest ordering the book one or more years in advance of the trip as the accommodations at these parks are limited and book up quickly.

The book is designed to eliminate the hours and hours of research for things to do on your vacation. When we used to travel, we would gather all of the brochures that looked interesting along the way. Most of which we just stacked up on a table in the corner of the room. Then we would pick things to do and wing it.

When we got home, we had more of a chance to review some of the information that we picked up. Then we would say, "I wish we would have known that special event was going on; it looks great."

This planning guide will eliminate those things from happening by determining what is important to you to see and do. The ebook is portable on your iPhone, Android, iPad, tablet, or laptop. As you see things of interest, you will have the website, phone number, and description at your fingertips, and you can check them out and also get reviews to help you plan.

<u>This book will help you identify:</u>

Lodging and Campgrounds in the park
Campgrounds near the park
Hiking Trails in the park
Tours in the park
Personal Recommendations
Local Attractions
Restaurants
Local area tours

Even though I am focusing my books on the National Parks and National Monuments, there is so much more than the National Park Service provides for us to visit and explore. These include:

National Battlefields (11) National Battlefields Parks (4)
National Battlefields Site (1) National Military Parks (9)
National Historic Parks (50) National Historic Sites (78)
International Historic Sites (1)National Lakeshores (4)
National Memorials (30) National Monuments (84)
National Parks (59) National Parkways (4)
National Preserves (19) National Reserves (2)
National Recreation Areas (18) National Rivers (5)
National Wild and Scenic Rivers and Riverways (10)
National Scenic Trails (3) National Seashores (10)
Other Designations (11)

Total of 413 as of August 24, 2016

Information on Park Passes:

A summary of park pass options are provided below. For more detailed information, please visit the National Park Service website: https://www.nps.gov/planyourvisit/passes.htm.

4th Grade Pass - This pass is valid for the duration of the 4th grade school year. This free pass for the 4th grader admits the entire family. Here are some of the details about the program.

- Cost: Free (valid for the duration of the 4th grade school year though the following summer (September-August)

- Available for: U.S. 4th graders (including home-schooled and free-choice learners 10 years of age) with a valid Every Kid in a Park paper pass

How to obtain:

- Paper passes can be obtained by visiting the Every Kid in a Park website and can be exchanged for the Annual 4th Grade Pass at federal recreation sites that charge Entrance or Standard Amenity fees (Day Use Fee) (see PDF list of federal recreation sites that issue passes).

- Digital version of the paper pass (such as on smart phones or tablets) will not be accepted to exchange for an Annual 4th Grade Pass.

- More information:
    - Non-transferable.
    - Educators can also be involved! Learn more at the Every Kid in a Park website.
    - Additional Details about the Annual 4th Grade Pass (USGS website)

Senior Pass - $80.00; (aka Golden Age or Golden Access Passports) is an interagency lifetime pass that admits the owner and up to three members "that arrive in the same vehicle."

Military Pass - FREE for those while on active duty and includes the owner and up to three members "that arrive in the same vehicle."

Park Annual Pass - There are no entrance fees for Biscayne National Park and Dry Tortugas has a $10 seven day pass.

Interagency Annual Pass - $80; is an annual pass that admits the owner and up to three members "that arrive in the same vehicle." This pass allows up to two different owners, who must sign the back of the pass.

Permanent disability - FREE and includes the owner and up to three guests "that arrive in the same vehicle."

"A pass is your ticket to more than 2,000 federal recreation sites. Each pass covers entrance fees at national parks and national wildlife refuges as well as standard amenity fees (day use fees) at national forests and grasslands and lands managed by the Bureau of Land Management, Bureau of Reclamation, and U.S. Army Corps of Engineers. A pass covers entrance, standard amenity fees, and day use fees for a driver and all passengers in a personal vehicle at per vehicle fee areas (or up to four adults at sites that charge per person). Children age 15 or under are admitted free."

Since things change frequently, please check the website for updates to the current/future editions for the latest information at NationalParkPlanningGuides.com under the Revisions tab. If you send me your email address, I will email them to you when changes occur. Positive reviews on Amazon are always helpful, and if you have any suggestions or additional information that would be helpful, please leave a comment on my website.

Additional information on Park Passes:

A pass is your ticket to more than 2,000 federal recreation sites. Each pass covers entrance fees at national parks and national wildlife refuges as well as standard amenity fees (day use fees) at national forests and grasslands and at lands managed by the Bureau of Land Management, Bureau of Reclamation, and U.S. Army Corps of Engineers. A pass covers entrance, standard amenity fees, and day use fees for a driver and all passengers in a personal vehicle at per vehicle fee areas (or up to four adults at sites that charge per person). Children age 15 or under are admitted free.

In most cases it is less expensive for a family to purchase an annual pass if you are planning to visit more than a couple of National Monuments or National Parks. One option is to purchase an annual pass and visit multiple times in that year to lower the cost per visit. With the NPS annual pass, I can assure you and your family will enjoy your visits to America's treasures. Thank you, and have a great adventure.

CONTENTS

1 TRANSPORTATION

Transportation for Biscayne and Dry Tortugas are the same. The major airports are Miami International Airport, Ft. Lauderdale International Airport, and Key West Airport. There is no Amtrak service to the Key West. I personally like the drive to Key West with great views along the way.

Estimated distance and driving times

Airport	To	Mile/Km	Time
Ft. Lauderdale Intl. Airport	Miami Intl Airport	26 miles / 42 km	35 min.
Ft. Lauderdale Intl. Airport	Biscayne National Park	64 miles / 103 km	1 hr. 15 min.
Ft. Lauderdale Intl. Airport	Key West	188 miles / 303 km	3 hrs. 50 min.
Miami Intl. Airport	Biscayne National Park	34 miles / 55 km	49 min.
Miami Intl. Airport	Key West	159 miles / 256 km	3 hrs. 23 min.
Key West Airport	Biscayne National Park	135 miles / 217 km	2 hrs. 58 min.

Key West International Airport (EYW) Website: http://www.broward.org/airport/Pages/Default.aspx

If your plans are to fly to Key West, you may want to consider using one of four carriers who have service to Key West. Otherwise, here is the connection information for each carrier where they originate. If you don't mind changing carriers and you land at Ft. Lauderdale change planes to Silver Airways, or Miami on American Airlines. Listed below are their connecting cities.

American - Miami, Washington National and Charlotte (seasonal)
Delta - Atlanta
Silver - Fort Lauderdale, Fort Meyers, Orlando and Tampa
United - Newark and Chicago O'Hare (both seasonal)

Airlines

Airline	Reservations	Website
American Airlines	800 433-7300	https://www.aa.com/homePage.do
Delta	800 221-1212	https://www.delta.com
Silver Airways	801-401-9100	https://www.silverairways.com
United	800-864-8331	https://www.united.com/ual/en/us/?root=1

Rental Cars

	Reservations	Website
Alamo (off site)	800 462-5266	https://www.alamo.com/en_US/car-rental/home.html
Avis	800 331-1212	https://www.avis.com/en/home
Budget	800 257-0700	https://www.budget.com/en/home
Dollar	800 800-4000	https://www.dollar.com
Enterprise (off site)	800 325-8007	https://www.enterprise.com/en/home.html
Hertz	800 654-3131	https://www.hertz.com/rentacar/reservation/
National (off site)	800 227-7368	https://www.nationalcar.com/en_US/car-rental/home.html
Thrifty	800 367-2277	https://www.thrifty.com

Miami International Airport (MIA) Website: http://www.miami-airport.com

The Miami Airport is one of the largest and busiest airports in the United States. However, offers most airlines that we all use. Make sure that you add a little extra time when departing as the baggage handling is in a separate area.

Airlines

Airline	Reservations	Website
Aeroflot	888-340-6400	http://www.aeroflot.com/ru-en
Aer Lingus	800-474-7424	https://www.aerlingus.com/html/en-US/home.html
Aerolineas Argentinas	800-333-0276	http://www.aerolineas.com.ar/Welcome
Aeromexico	800-237-6639	https://aeromexico.com/es-mx/
Air Canada	888-247-2262	https://www.aircanada.com/us/en/aco/home.html
Air Europa	800-238-7672	https://www.aireuropa.com/en/flights
Air France	800-237-2747	https://www.airfrance.com/indexCom_en.html
Air Italy	718 751 4499	https://www.airitaly.com/en/
Alitalia	800-223-5730	https://www.alitalia.com/en_us
American Airlines	800 433-7300	https://www.aa.com/homePage.do
Aruba Airlines		
Austrian Airlines	800-843-0002	https://www.austrian.com
Avianca	800-284-2622	https://www.avianca.com/co/es/
Avior Airlines	305-470-2203	https://www.aviorair.com
Bahamasair	800-222-4262	https://www.bahamasair.com
BOA	305-591-3217	http://www.boa.bo/BoAWebSite/
British Airways	800-247-9297	https://www.caribbean-airlines.com/#/main
Caribbean Airlines	800-538-2942	https://www.caribbean-airlines.com/#/main

Airline	Reservations	Website
Cayman Airways	800-422-9626	https://www.caymanairways.com
COPA Airlines	800-359-2672	https://www.copaair.com/en/web/us
Delta	800 221-1212	https://www.delta.com
El Al	800-223-6700	https://www.elal.com/en/USA/Pages/default.aspx
Eurowings	845-709-8332	https://www.eurowings.com/en.html
Finnair	800-950-5000	https://www.finnair.com/int/gb/
Frontier Airlines	801-401-9000	https://www.flyfrontier.com
Iberia	800-772-4642	https://www.iberia.com
Interjet	866-285-9525	https://www.interjet.com/Home.aspx
KLM	00-618-0104	https://www.klm.com
LATAM Airlines	866-435-9526	https://www.latam.com/en_us/
Lufthansa	800-645-3880	https://www.lufthansa.com/online/portal/lh/us/homepage
Miami Air	305-876-3600	http://www.miamiair.com
Qatar	877-777-2827	https://www.qatarairways.com/en-us/homepage.html
SAS		https://www.flysas.com/us-en/
Sun Country	800-359-6786	https://www.suncountry.com/booking/search.html
Surinam Airways	305-599-1196	http://www.slm.nl/?EN/1
Swiss International	877-359-7947	https://www.swiss.com/us/en
TAP Air Portugal	800-221-7370	https://www.flytap.com/en-us/
Thomas Cook	866-960-7915	https://www.thomascook.com
TUIfly	855-808-4015	https://en.tuifly.com
Turkish	800-874-8875	https://www.turkishairlines.com

Airline	Reservations	Website
United	800-874-8875	https://www.united.com/ual/en/us/?root=1
Virgin Atlantic	800-862-8621	https://www.virginatlantic.com/us/en
VivaAir	844-569-7126	https://vivaair.com/co
Volaris	844-569-7126	https://www.volaris.com
WestJet	888-937-8538	https://www.westjet.com/en-ca/index
World Atlantic	305-722-6100	http://flywaa.com/#tf-home
XL Airways France		https://www.xl.com/en
Xtra Airways	876-34-4433	http://xtraairways.com

Rental Cars

	Reserve	Local	Website
Advantage Rent A Car	800 777-5500	305 874-2135	https://www.advantage.com
Alamo	800 327-9633	305 633-6076	https://www.alamo.com/en_US/car-rental/home.html
Avis	800 331-1212	305 341-0936	https://www.avis.com/en/home
Budget	800 257-0700	305 871-2722	https://www.budget.com/en/home
Dollar	800 800-4000	866 434-2226	https://www.dollar.com
Enterprise	800 325-8007	305 633-0377	https://www.enterprise.com/en/home.html
E-Z Rent A Car	800 277-5171	305 635-3230	https://www.e-zrentacar.com
Hertz	800 654-3131	305 871-0300	https://www.hertz.com/rentacar/reservation/
National	800 227-7368	305 638-1026	https://www.nationalcar.com/en_US/car-rental/home.html
Payless	800 729-5377	305 870-0397	https://www.paylesscar.com/en/home
P&P Family Auto Rental	800 531-1177	305 638-9400	http://www.familyautorental.com
Royal	800 314-8616	305 871-3000	https://www.royalrentacar.com
Sixt Rent A Car	888 749-8227	305 503-9849	https://www.sixt.com
Thrifty	800 367-2277	800 367-2277	https://www.thrifty.com

Ft. Lauderdale International Airport (FLL) Website: http://www.broward.org/airport/Pages/Default.aspx

Airlines

Airline	Reservations	Website
Air Canada	888-247-2262	https://www.aircanada.com/us/en/aco/home.html
Air Transat	877-872-6728	https://www.airtransat.com
AirTran Airways	800-435-9792	https://www.southwest.com/?ref=airtrain.com
Alaska Airlines	800-252-7522	https://www.alaskaair.com
Allegiant	702-505-8888	https://www.allegiantair.com
American Airlines	800 433-7300	https://www.aa.com/homePage.do
Avianca	800-284-2622	https://www.avianca.com/co/es/
Avianca Airlines	800-284-2622	https://www.avianca.com/us/en/
Azul Airlines	844-499-2985	https://www.voeazul.com.br/en
Bahamasair	800-222-4262	https://www.bahamasair.com
British Airways	800-247-9297	https://www.caribbean-airlines.com/#/main
Caribbean Airlines	800-920-4225	https://www.caribbean-airlines.com/#/main
COPA Airlines	800-359-2672	https://www.copaair.com/en/web/us
Delta	800 221-1212	https://www.delta.com
Emirates Airline	800- 777-3999	https://www.emirates.com/us/english/
Florida Coastal Airlines	954-772-9808	http://www.flyfca.net
IBC Airways	954-834-1700	http://www.ibcairways.com
JetBlue Airways	800-538-2583	https://www.jetblue.com
Norwegian Air Shuttle	800-357-4159	https://www.norwegian.com/uk/invisible-pages/norwegiancom/

Airline	Reservations	Website
Silver Airways	801-401-9100	https://www.silverairways.com
Skybahamas Airlines	954-357-0696	http://skybahamas.net
Southwest Airlines	800-435-9792	https://www.southwest.com/?ref=southwestairlines.com
Spirit Airlines	801-401-2222	https://www.spirit.com
Sun Air International	877-226-2040	http://www.gosunair.com
Sunwing Airlines	877-786-9464	https://www.sunwing.ca/pages/en/sunwing-airlines
TAME Airlines	855-701-7244	https://www.tame.com.ec/index.php/en/
United	800-523-3273	https://www.united.com/ual/en/us/?root=1
WestJet	888-937-8538	https://www.westjet.com/en-ca/index

Rental Cars

	Reservations	Website
Advantage Rent A Car	800 777-5500	https://www.advantage.com
Alamo	800 462-5266	https://www.alamo.com/en_US/car-rental/home.html
Avis	800 331-1212	https://www.avis.com/en/home
Budget	800 218-7992	https://www.budget.com/en/home
Dollar	800 800-4000	https://www.dollar.com
Enterprise	800 325-8007	https://www.enterprise.com/en/home.html
E-Z Rent A Car	800 277-5171	https://www.e-zrentacar.com
Hertz	800 654-3131	https://www.hertz.com/rentacar/reservation/
National	800 227-7368	https://www.nationalcar.com/en_US/car-rental/home.html
Payless	800 729-5377	https://www.paylesscar.com/en/home
Royal	800 314-8616	https://www.royalrentacar.com
Thrifty	800 847-4389	https://www.thrifty.com

2 DRY TORTUGAS OVERVIEW

Courtyard of Fort Jefferson

Dry Tortugas became a National Park on October 26, 1992. The park covers approximately 64,701.22 acres (261.8 km2). It is located in southern Florida approximately 69 miles west of Key West, FL and was visited by 54,281 visitors in 2017. There are two Visitor Centers, one on Garden Key located inside of Fort Jefferson and the other at the Florida Keys Eco Discovery Center. For more information the Florida Keys Eco Discovery Center see the following website: http://floridakeys.noaa.gov/eco_discovery.html

- **Contact Information:** 40001 SR-9336, Homestead, FL 33034
- **Website:** https://www.nps.gov/drto/index.htm
- **Physical Address:** Use GPS coordinates
- **Phone number:** (305) 242-7700
- **GPS Coordinates:** 24° 37' 39" N, 82° 52' 19" W
- **ADA Accessibility:** The visitor center is accessible; however, the trails are not recommended due to the terrain variations.

• **Admission Fee:** $10 per person which is priced into the ferry ticket price, and if you have a National Park Pass the $10 will be refunded by the National Park boat tour company. (See the Information on Park Passes section of "How to use the Planning Guide").

• **Hours:** Open every day, 24 hours a day.

• **Pet Information:** Pets are permitted on Garden Key, but are prohibited inside Fort Jefferson. Pets must be kept on a six foot leash.

• **Passport Stamp Location**: Just as you enter the bookstore.

Dry Tortugas is unique from the other National Parks. It is the southernmost park and is approximately 69 miles west of Key West Florida. The Islands have no fresh water from the ground, and, with the exception of some primitive camping, no one lives on the islands.

Cover photo of Fort Jefferson

There is a small book store, but it does not sell food or drink. For those taking the Ferry (Yankee Freedom II), breakfast and lunch will be served, and they have a galley for the ride home (which even serves beer and wine and snacks) for the ride back to Key West. As part of the ticket they provide optional snorkel equipment on the island. The park ferry is the most affordable option, and the crew and tour guide was great. The Yankee Freedom II is a 110 foot high speed catamaran. On our journey there were several people on the bow of the ship that saw sea turtles. At Fort Jefferson a few of the guests did see a nine foot saltwater crocodile that has been hanging out there for many years and also some very large birds called the magnificent Frigate bird, with up to a 40 inch wing span and only weighing about 3 lbs. Remember to make sure you bring plenty of sun screen for the trip, as many of the guests spent most of the time out on the deck enjoying the Florida sunshine!

Don't forget that you can also camp overnight at the island.

If you drive in from the mainland, your journey starts at mile marker (MM) 113, on what is known as the "Overseas Highway". The Overseas Highway connects islands and keys between Mainland Florida with Key West. The longest bridge is 6.79 miles long, with the highest point of 65 feet at Moser Channel. As you travel down the highway you may notice what appears to be railroad tracks, and you would be correct. Henry Flagler, who was the builder of the Florida East Coast Railroad that extended from Jacksonville to Miami, decided he wanted to extend it to Key West. They said it couldn't be done, and with his own personal funds he built the extension that was completed in 1912. The railroad was used until the Labor Day Hurricane of 1935. They did not have the funds to rebuild it, so they ended up selling the bridges and land that was not destroyed by the hurricane to Florida. The MM is the golden standard for talking with the locals to determine where a particular restaurant, campground, or attraction is located if it is not located on the island of Key West.

The temperature ranges from 92 in the summer to 70s in the winter, with very little rainfall on the keys. Peak seasons for Key West and Dry Tortugas are from Christmas to mid-April.

If you are planning to visit Dry Tortugas National Park you will most likely be spending some time in Key West, Florida. You may fly directly into the Key West International Airport or maybe take the meandering ride down Florida scenic route US1 from Miami down to Key West.

Historical Temperatures for Dry Tortugas National Park:

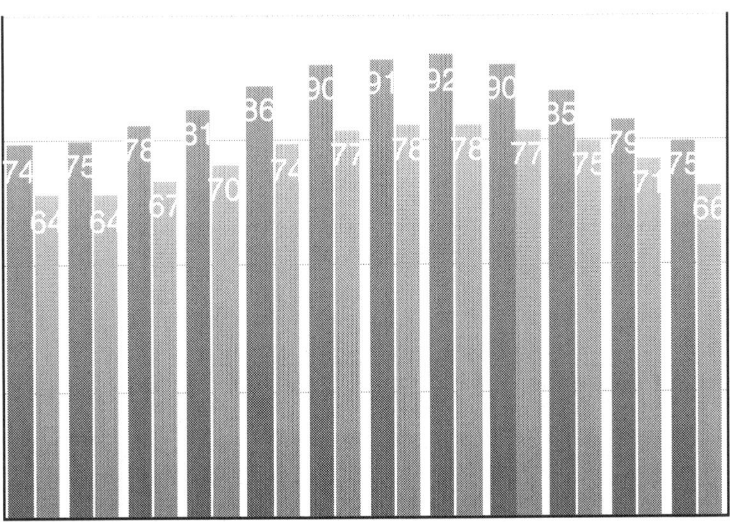

Jan Feb Mar Apr May Jun Jul Aug Sep Oct Nov Dec

Average Temperature for Dry Tortugas National Park

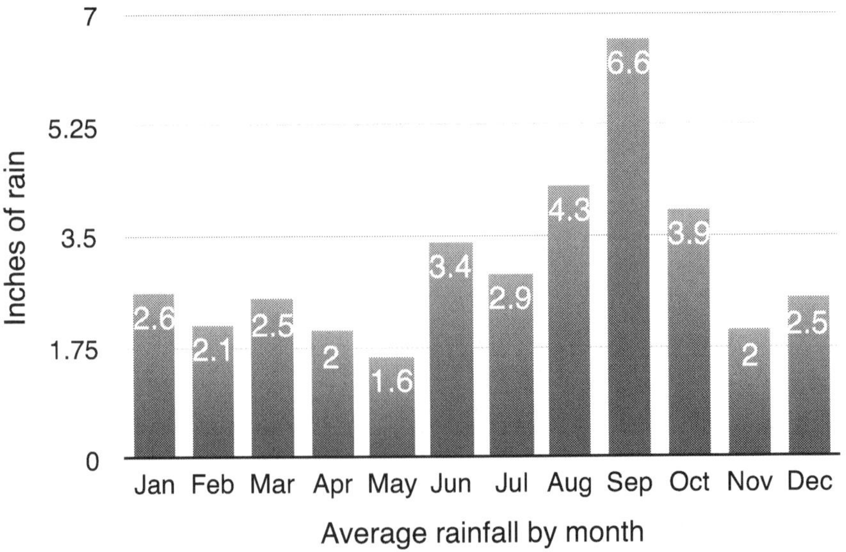

Average rainfall by month

Source: Weather-us.com

3 DRY TORTUGAS HISTORY

Dry Tortugas is made up of seven small islands approximately 69 miles west of Key West Florida. The islands got the first part of its name, Tortugas, when Juan Ponce De Leon found the islands in 1513. There were approximately 200 turtles on the shore and so he named the island Tortugas or "Turtle". Later "Dry" was added to the maps to identify that the island had no fresh water to the boating navigation charts. Source: NPS

Passage way on the North wall

The first structure was a lighthouse that was built on the Garden Island in 1825. It was one of the first lighthouses in the United States and helped the ships navigate near the shore without running aground. Later in 1856 they made a taller one that stood 150 feet tall. In 1912 it was automated and became unmanned. By 1924 the lighthouse had seen the end of its useful life and was decommissioned.

Fort Jefferson is the largest brick masonry and fortified fort in North America. The construction has over 16 million bricks and was started in 1846. Construction continued for almost 30 years but was never completed. The fort is one of the more accessible forts, and you walk totally around the moat and each of the three floors.

The fort was originally built the federal government and was the southernmost Union Army stronghold. The fort, during its peak use, held approximately 1,500 people. It was used as the prison for Union deserters. When Abraham Lincoln was assassinated in the 1865, the four men convicted of complicity were also imprisoned there along with Dr. Mudd, another key figure.

- By 1874 the United States Army left the fort, never to return.

- In 1908 it became wildlife refuge to the protect the sooty tern rookery birds.

- In 1935 it became a National Monument.

- In 1992 Dry Tortugas became a National Park.

There are four ways to visit Dry Tortugas. First, the Jefferson Ferry offers daily trips between the islands and Key West. Second, the seaplane shuttle, also running between the islands and Key West. Third, take a private charter or private boat to make the crossing to the islands. And fourth would be to bring your own boat.

4 DRY TORTUGAS ACTIVITIES

Just Relaxing

Dry Tortugas is a great place to relax and enjoy the beauty of nature. The water, no matter which direction you look, contains shades of green aqua and blue. It usually has a nice sea breeze, but I did locate a natural air conditioner on the island. As you walk into the fort through the sally port door, stand a moment and the cool air there is refreshing.

Snorkeling

There are only two areas that swimming and snorkeling is permitted on the key, and they are the North Beach and the South Beach. Even with the visitors from the Ferry and seaplanes that come there, usually the beaches are pretty much uninhabited. And for the campers, after the tours are gone the key is yours.

Swimming beach on the right

Semi-private beach

Even with the tours on the key, you will find both the north and south beaches pretty private, as most of the guests from the tours are out looking around.

Photography
Photographing on this key provides many unique opportunities for some great shots.

Frigate bird overhead

Birding
Let me admit up front that I love looking at all of the unique birds and their colors, the way they soar and walk. While I was at the fort I did see many different types of birds, some I was able to figure out and others I couldn't. The most prominent bird on the key was the Frigate bird, and the community when they weren't flying were on a little island maybe 1/4 mile away.

Exploring
We enjoyed exploring the fort, and we were amazed at just how large it truly was. It is hard to imagine how hard it must have been to construct such a structure. With the thought and engineering that went into capturing rain water, to the design of the walls to be able to withstand the recoil of enormous cannons. The NPS has interpretive signs as you walk along the self-guided tour.

Star gazing
To be able to properly gaze into the heavens you need no lights around you,

and Dry Tortugas is the one place that you can experience star gazing at its finest.

Watching Sunrise / Sunsets
Dry Tortugas offers a truly unique experience to watch a non-obstructed sunrise, and at the end of the day watch a non-obstructed sunset.

Kayaking
Kayaking is a way to get around to some of the areas around the park with, like the loggerhead key and the Windjammer wreck. The only way that I found to get a kayak over to Dry Tortugas is by private boat charter or by the National Park Ferry.

5 DRY TORTUGAS ACCOMMODATIONS

Camping Overview

Camping on the Garden Key will be different from any other camping experience that you may have had. While on the key you may see some beautiful sunrises and/or sunsets, star gazing, plenty of snorkeling, birding, and exploring the fort.

All of those things come at a very small price... And that is that you must bring everything that you need for the number of days that you will be camping (food, water, etc.) and that everything you bring in, you pack out.

Open flames are not permitted; however if you bring a gas stove or charcoal briquettes they are permitted if used inside of an established campsite BBQ unit.

Camping in the park

Remember you must bring everything including water.

The NPS has a great brochure with camping information. https://www.nps.gov/drto/planyourvisit/upload/campingdrto.pdf and also the general information at: https://www.nps.gov/drto/planyourvisit/camping.htm

6 KEY WEST OVERVIEW

This is an assumption on my part. And I know I have always been told to never assume… But here goes anyway. Most visitors of Dry Tortugas National Park will spend some time on Key West.

And that is the reason that I put in all the things that see and do in this island paradise.

You will find that Key West is a very dog-friendly place, with bowls of water out from of many of the shops for dogs as they stroll by.

Key West is well known for their nightlife, especially on Duvall street.

There are many festivals in Key West that are family oriented. However, the Fantasy Fest is not one of them. It is an adult venue that lasts ten days of costuming, parades, libations and filled with excitement. The 2018 dates are from October 19-28. For information, here is their website: http://www.fantasyfest.com

7 KEY WEST ACCOMMODATIONS

Local Campgrounds

There are many terrific campgrounds near Key West. Most are near the water and some with marinas. The keys use "Mile Markers" as there address (e.g., MM 4 = mile marker 4).

Listed below are brief descriptions for each of the campgrounds with the details on some of the amenities:

Name	Address	Phone (305)	Website	
Leo's Campground	MM 4.5	296-5260	http:// leoscampground.com	C, W
Boyd's Key West Campground	MM5	294-1465	https:// www.boydscampground.com	C, W, PO,
El Mar Campground	MM5	294-0857	http:// www.elmarrvresort.com	C, W, B,
Sugarloaf Key KOA	MM 20	745-3549	http:// www.sugarloafkeykoa.com	C, W, PO
Bluewater Key RV Resort	MM 14.5	745-2494	http:// www.bluewaterkey.com	R
Geiger Key Marina & RV Park	MM 10.5	296-3553	http:// www.geigerkeymarina.com	
Lazy Lakes RV Resort	MM 14	745-1079	http:// www.lazylakeskeyscamping.com	C, W, PO

C=Cable, W=Wifi, B=Big Rigs, PU=Pull-Thru, PL=Playground,

PO=Pool, S=Store, R=Rentals

Local Hotels

Name	Address	Phone (305)	Website
Key West Marriott Beachside Hotel	3841 N Roosevelt Blvd	296-8100	http://www.marriott.com/hotels/travel/eywmc-key-west-marriott-beachside-hotel/?scid=bb1a189a-fec3-4d19-a255-54ba596febe2
Double Tree Resort - Grand Key	3990 S Roosevelt Blvd	293-1818	http://doubletree3.hilton.com/en/hotels/florida/doubletree-resort-by-hilton-hotel-grand-key-key-west-EYWDTDT/index.html
Fairfield Inn & Suites	2400 N Roosevelt Blvd	296-5700	http://www.marriott.com/hotels/travel/eywfi-fairfield-inn-and-suites-key-west/?scid=bb1a189a-fec3-4d19-a255-54ba596febe2
La Concha Hotel & Spa	430 Duval Street	296-2991	http://www.laconchakeywest.com
Sheraton Suites	2001 S Roosevelt Blvd	292-9800	http://www.sheratonkeywest.com
Best Western Key Ambassador Resort Inn	3755 S Roosevelt Blvd	296-3500	https://www.bestwestern.com/en_US/book/hotel-details.10011.html?iata=00171880&ssob=BLBWI0004G&cid=BLBWI0004G:google:gmb:10011
Parrot Key Hotel and Resort	2801 N Roosevelt Blvd	600-0097	http://www.parrotkeyresort.com/

Name	Address	Phone (305)	Website
Courtyard by Marriott Key West Waterfront	3031-41 N Roosevelt Blvd	296-6595	http://www.marriott.com/hotels/travel/eywcy-courtyard-key-west-waterfront/?scid=bb1a189a-fec3-4d19-a255-54ba596febe2
Hyatt Centric Key West Resort & Spa	601 Front Street	809-1234	https://keywest.centric.hyatt.com/en/hotel/home.html
Southernmost Beach Resort	508 South Street	296-6577	http://www.southernmostbeachresort.com
The Saint Hotel Key West, Autograph Collection	417 Eaton Street	294-3200	http://www.marriott.com/hotels/travel/eywak-the-saint-hotel-key-west--autograph-collection/?scid=bb1a189a-fec3-4d19-a255-54ba596febe2
Best Western Hibiscus Motel	1313 Simonton Street	294-3763	https://www.bestwestern.com/en_US/book/hotel-details.10206.html?iata=00171880&ssob=BLBWI0004G&cid=BLBWI0004G:google:gmb:10206
North Hotel	3820 N Roosevelt Blvd	320-0940	https://www.24northhotel.com
Casa Marina Resort The Waldorf Astoria Collection	1500 Reynolds Street	296-3535	http://waldorfastoria3.hilton.com/en/hotels/florida/casa-marina-a-waldorf-astoria-resort-EYWCMWA/index.html
The Gardens Hotel	526 Angela Street	294-2661	http://www.gardenshotel.com

Bed & Breakfast Inns

If you are looking for fun and excitement in your trip to Key West, you may want to stay near Duval Street and Mallory Square. This is where most of the restaurants and night time activities take place. If you want to camp at one of campgrounds, there is public transportation that is very reasonable and will take you down town and back to the campground. Consult the online bus schedule for locations of their stops and time schedule. Make sure to allow extra time since on the keys the average speed south of mile marker 50 is approximately 30 to 35 MPH depending on traffic.
Listed below are the Bed and Breakfasts in Key West..

Name	Address	Phone (305)	Website
Ambrosia Key West	622 Fleming Street	296-9838	www.ambrosiakeywest.com
An Island Oasis	630 South Street	296-4275	www.anislandoasis.com
Andrews Inn and Garden Cottages	223 Eanes Lane	294-7730	www.andrewsinn.com
Angelina Guest House	302 Angela Street	294-4480	www.angelinaguesthouse.com
Artist House	534 Eaton Street	296-3977	www.artisthousekeywest.com
Atlantis House	1401 Atlantic Blvd.	292-1532	www.atlantishouse.com
Artist House on Fleming	1016 Fleming Street	294-4043	www.artisthouseonfleming.com
Authors Of Key West Guesthouse	725 White Street	294-7381	www.authorskeywest.com
Avalon Bed & Breakfast	1317 Duval Street	294-8233	www.avalonbnb.com
Azul Key West	907 Truman Avenue	296-5152	www.azulkeywest.com

Name	Address	Phone (305)	Website
Blue Parrot Inn	916 Elizabeth Street	296-0033	www.blueparrotinn.com
Coconut Beach Resort	1500 Alberta Street	294-0057	www.coconutbeachresort.com
Coco Plum Inn	611 Whitehead Street	295-2955	www.cocopluminn.com
Conch House Heritage Inn	625 Truman Avenue	293-0020	http://conchhouse.com
Courtney's Place	720 Whitmarsh Lane	294-3480	www.courtneysplacekeywest.com
Curry House	806 Fleming Street	294-6777	www.curryhousekeywest.com
Cypress House	601 Caroline Street	294-6969	www.historickeywestinn.com
Duval Gardens	1012 Duval Street	(800) 867-1234	www.duvalgardens.com
Duval Inn	511 Angela Street	(877) 418-6900	www.duvalinn.com
Eden House	1015 Fleming Street	296-6868	www.edenhouse.com
Frances Street Bottle Inn	535 Frances Street	294-8530	www.bottleinn.com
Garden House	329 Elizabeth Street	296-5368	www.the-garden-house.com
Gardens Hotel	526 Angela Street	294-2661	www.gardenshotel.com

Name	Address	Phone (305)	Website
Island City House			
Key West Bed And Breakfast	415 William Street	296-7274	www.keywestbandb.com
Key West Harbor Inn	219 Elizabeth Street	296-0898	www.keywestharborinn.com
Knowles House	1004 Eaton Street	(800) 352-4414	www.knowleshouse.com
La Mer/ Dewey House	506 South Street	296-6577	www.southernmostresort.com
La Pensione Inn	809 Truman Avenue	292-9923	www.lapensione.com
L'Habitation	408 Eaton Street	293-9203	www.lhabitation.com
Mango Tree Inn	603 Southard Street	293-1177	www.mangotree-inn.com
Marrero's Guest Mansion	410 Fleming Street	294-6977	http://marreros.com
Merlin Guesthouse	811 Simonton Street	296-3336	http://www.historickeywestinns.com/the-inns/merlin-guesthouse/
Mermaid & The Alligator	729 Truman Ave	294-1894	www.kwmermaid.com
Old Customs House Inn	124 Duval Street	294-8507	www.oldcustomshouse.com
Old Town Manor	511 Eaton Street	292-2170	www.oldtownmanor.com

Name	Address	Phone (305)	Website
Paradise Inn	819 Simonton Street	293-8007	www.theparadiseinn.com
Pilot House	414 Simonton Street	293-6600	www.pilothousekeywest.com
Rose Lane Villas	522 Rose Lane	292-2170	www.roselanevillas.com
Seaport Inn Of Key West	329 William Street	(800) 869-4639	http://www.seaportinnkeywest.com/seaportinnkeywestpolicies.htm
Seascape Tropical Inn	420 Olivia Street	296-7776	www.seascapetropicalinn.com
Southernmost Point Guest House	1400 Duval Street	296-3141	www.southernmosthouse.com
The Grand Guesthouse	1116 Grinnell Street	294-0590	www.thegrandguesthouse.com
Travelers Palm Inn & Cottages	815 Catherine Street	302-1751	www.travlerspalm.com
Tropical Inn	812 Duval Street	(888) 611-6510	www.tropicalinn.com
Weatherstation Inn	57 Front Street	294-7277	www.weatherstationinn.com
Wicker Guesthouse	913 Duval Street	296-4275	http://keywesthospitalityinns.com

8 KEY WEST RESTAURANTS

Websites I used for doing a quick check on restaurants and ratings are listed below:

- https://www.tripadvisor.com/Restaurants
- www.foodandwine.com/restaurants
- https://www.zagat.com
- https://www.yelp.com/

The restaurants in Key West are all unique, and I have never found one that I didn't like. Since I live in Florida, I usually go for the local seafood. Even though I have provided you with most of them in the historic area, I would encourage you to check the ratings before you go. Here are a couple of my favorites: A&B Lobster House- more upscale, Two Sister - moderate price great atmosphere, Blue Have, if you can get in, or the Blue Macaw, and of course Better Than Sex - deserts served with an adult flair. Sloppy Joe's, Hogsbreath, or Margaritaville for bar food, of course there are another 80 to pick from.

Name	Type	Address	Phone	Website
A&B Lobster House	SF	700 Front St	294-5880	http://aandblobsterhouse.com
Azur Restaurant	ME	425 Grinnell St	292-2987	http://www.azurkeywest.com
Bad Boy Burrito	ME	1128 Simonton St	292-2697	http://www.badboyburrito.com
Banana Cafe	FR	1215 Duval St	294-7227	http://www.bananacafekw.com
Better Than Sex	DE	926 Simonton St	296-8102	http://www.betterthansexkeywest.com

Name	Type	Address	Phone	Website
Blackfin Bistro	**GR**	918 Duval St	509-7408	http://www.blackfinbistro.com
Bliss Restaurant	**SF**	411 Petronia St	240-1281	http://www.blissrestaurantkw.com
Blue Heaven	**FL**	729 Thomas St	296-8666	http://www.blueheavenkw.com
Blue Macaw Island Eats	**FL**	804 Whitehead St	440-3196	http://www.bluemacawkeywest.com
Cafe Sole	**ME**	1029 Southard St	294-0230	http://www.cafesole.com
Camille's Key West	**AM**	1202 Simonton St	296-4811	http://www.camilleskeywest.com
Commodore Waterfront	**SF**	700 Front St	294-9191	http://www.commodorekeywest.com
Conch Republic Seafood	**SF**	631 Greene St	294-4403	https://www.conchrepublicseafood.com
Cuban Coffee Queen	**CS**	284 Margaret St	292-4747	http://www.cubancoffeequeen.com
Date and Thyme	**VE**	829 Fleming St	296-7766	http://www.helpyourselffoods.com
Denny's	**AM**	925 Duval St	294-5065	https://locations.dennys.com/FL/KEY-WEST/247346?utm_source=yext&utm_medium=local-listing&utm_campaign=yext-listing

Name	Type	Address	Phone	Website
Deuces "Off The Hook" Grill	**GR**	728 Simonton St	414-8428	http://www.offthehookkeywest.com
DJ's Clam Shack	**SF**	629 Duval St	294-0102	http://djsclamshack.com
Duffy's Steak & Lobster House	**SF**	1007 Simonton	296-4900	http://www.duffyskeywest.com
El Siboney	**CU**	900 Catherine St	296-4184	http://www.elsiboneyrestaurant.com
Fogarty's	**AM**	227 Duval St	294-7525	http://fogartysofkeywest.com
Garbo's Grill	**GR**	409 Caroline St	304-3004	http://www.garbosgrillkw.com
HarborView Cafe	**AM**	1 Duval St	296-4600	https://www.pierhouse.com
Hard Rock Café		231 Margaret St	294-7496	http://www.halfshellrawbar.com
Hog's Breath Saloon	**BR**	400 Front St	296-4222	https://www.hogsbreath.com
Hong Kong Restaurant	**CI**	2804 N Roosevelt Blvd	296-8608	http://www.keywestchinesefood.com
Hot Tin Roof	**FD**	0 Duval St	295-7057	http://www.oceankey.com/key-west-restaurant.aspx
Incas Restaurant	**PR**	800 White St	292-1616	http://incasrestaurant.wixsite.com/incasrestaurant

Name	Type	Address	Phone	Website
Jack Flats	AM	509 Duval St	294-7955	http://jackflatskw.com
La Trattoria	IT	524 Duval St	296-1075	http://latrattoria.us
Louie's Backyard	CR	700 Waddell Ave	294-1061	http://www.louiesbackyard.com
Mangia Mangia		900 Southard St	294-2469	http://www.mangia-mangia.com
Michaels Restaurant	AM	532 Margaret St	295-1300	http://www.michaelskeywest.com
New York Pasta Garden	IT	1075 Duval St	292-1991	http://www.newyorkpastagarden.com/index.html
Nine One Five	TA	915 Duval St	296-0669	https://www.915duval.com
Onlywood Pizzeria	PI	613-1/2 Duval St	735-4412	https://onlywoodkw.com
Pepe's	CA	806 Caroline St	294-7192	http://pepeskeywest.com
Pinchers	SF	712 Duval St	440-2179	http://www.pinchersusa.com/key-west.php
Red Fish Blue Fish	SF	407 Front St # 1	295-7447	http://redfishbluefishkw.com
Rooftop Cafe	AM	308 Front St	294-2042	http://www.rooftopcafekeywest.com
Rum Barrel	SB	528 Front St	292-7862	http://www.rumbarrel.com

Name	Type	Address	Phone	Website
Santiago's Bodega	ER	207 Petronia St #101	296-7691	http://www.santiagosbodega.com
Sarabeth's Kitchen	AM	530 Simonton St,	293-8181	http://sarabethskeywest.com
Schooner Wharf Bar	BR	202 William St	292-3302	http://www.schoonerwharf.com
Seven Fish	SF	921 Truman Ave	296-2777	http://www.7fish.com
Shor American Seafood Grill	SF	601 Front St	809-4000	http://www.shorgrill.com/hpr/shor/en/key_west.html
Sloppy Joe's	BR	201 Duval St	294-5717	https://sloppyjoes.com
Smokin' Tuna Saloon	GR	4 Charles St	517-6350	http://www.smokintunasaloon.com
Southern most Beach Cafe	CR	1405 Duval St	295-6550	http://www.southernmostbeachcafe.com
Two Friends Patio Restaurant	AM	512 Front St	296-3124	http://twofriendskeywest.com
Willie T's	BR	525 Duval St	294-7674	http://www.williets.com

AM= American, BR= Bar, CA= Cafe, CI= Chinese, CR= Caribbean, CS= Coffee Shop, CU= Cuban, DE= Deserts, ER= Eclectic Restaurant, FD=Fine Dining, FL= Floridian, FR= French, GR= Grill, IT= Italian, ME= Mediterranean, PI= Pizza, PR= Peruvian, SB= Sports Bar, TA= Tapas

9 KEY WEST ACTIVITIES

Contact information, website, telephone number, and basic information was correct at the time of this books release. However, since things do change, please contact any place that you plan to visit to make sure that the information is still correct.

The trolley tours are a great way to not only reduce the amount of walking, but they also provide a fully narrated tour along the way. You have a couple of options depending on where you are staying. First, if you are staying at any of the resorts on the east side of town the Old Town Trolley would be your best bet. The City View and the Conch Train stay in the Historic District with more information on the historic area. All of the trolleys are fully narrated, and they all do a great job. The online price for the City View was $18, but we ended up booking at stop one and we ended getting it for only $19. Since I have driven several touring companies I am a little more critical. Our guide was John from Iowa/Pennsylvania, and he was great and both knowledgeable and entertaining. City View offered other discount coupons for attractions while riding the trolley.

Here are some pictures of some of the free tourist attractions. One of the favorite spots is on “Sunset Pier” to watch the sunset. Both locals and tourist alike go for the evening viewing.

It can get pretty crowded so make sure that you get there at least a half an hour before sunset. The other two pictures are the Southernmost Point Bouy and the beginning of US 1 and mile marker 0.
Key West is loaded with lots and lots of water related activities, in addition to museums and many free things that you can visit.

Commercial Tours

Name	Address	Phone	Website
City View	105 Whitehead St	294-0644	http://www.cityviewtrolleys.com
Old Town Trolley Tours	Stop 1 is by Mallory Square	296-6688	http://www.trolleytours.com/key-west/
Conch Tour Train	Front Street depot by Mallory Square	(888) 916-8687	http://www.conchtourtrain.com/
Ghost Tours	Stop 1 is by Mallory Square	292-2040	http://www.trolleytours.com/key-west/
Lloyds Tropical Bike Tour	Corner of Truman Ave and Simonton St	304-4700	http://www.lloydstropicalbiketour.com
Sunset water sports	Various departure locations	296-2554	http://www.sunsetwatersportskeywest.com/index.html
Fury Water Adventures		294-8899	https://www.furycat.com/
Islescapes	202 William St., Key West, FL	923-3319	https://www.facebook.com/Islescapes-Key-West-Dinner-Cruises-and-Snorkeling-140371620148/
Pub Crawl & Haunted Pub Crawl	218 Whitehead Street Suite 2 Key West FL	294-7170	http://www.duvalcrawl.com
Seaplane Adventures	3471 South Roosevelt Boulevard, Key West, Fl	293-9300	https://keywestseaplanecharters.com
Water Tours	5106 US-1, Key West, FL	294-6790	http://keywestwatertours.com

Name	Address	Phone	Website
Key West Seaplanes	3471 S Roosevelt Blvd, Key West, FL	294-4014	http://www.keywestseaplanes.com

Sites to see

Name	$	Address	Phone	Website
Curry Mansion Museum	$	511 Caroline St	294-5349	http://www.conchrepublicgroup.com/dynamic/index.php?id=129
Dry Tortugas Visitor Center Key West	F	West's Seaport		https://www.nps.gov/drto/planyourvisit/the-bight-visitor-center.htm
Dry Tortugas Eco Discovery Center	F	33 E Quay Rd	809-4750	http://floridakeys.noaa.gov/eco_discovery.html
Ernest Hemingway Home and Museum	$	907 Whitehead St	294-1136	http://www.hemingwayhome.com
Ft Zachary Taylor Historic State Park	F	601 Howard England Way	292-6713	http://www.fortzacharytaylor.com
Key West Shipwreck Museum	$	1 Whitehead St	292-8990	https://www.keywestshipwreck.com
Key West Aquarium	$	1 Whitehead St	296-2051	https://www.keywestaquarium.com

Name	$	Address	Phone	Website
Truman Little White House	$	111 Front St	294-9911	https://www.trumanlittlewhitehouse.com
Customs House Museum	$	281 Front St	295-6616	http://www.kwahs.org/museums/custom-house/history
Mel Fisher's Maritime Museum	$	200 Greene St	294-2633	http://www.melfisher.org
Waterfront Playhouse	$	310 Wall St	394-7445	https://www.waterfrontplayhouse.org
Ripley's Believe It or Not!	$	108 Duval St	293-9939	http://www.ripleys.com/keywest/
Nancy Forrester's Secret Garden	$	518 Elizabeth St	294-0015	http://nancyforrester.com
Our Lady of Lourdes Shrine	F	1010 Windsor Ln	294-1018	http://www.stmarykeywest.com/about-our-parish/map-and-buildings/grotto/
Smathers Beach	F	S Roosevelt Blvd	809-3700	https://www.cityofkeywest-fl.gov/egov/apps/locations/facilities.egov?view=detail&id=24
Southermost Point	F	Corner of South and Whitehead	Just a Buoy	https://en.wikipedia.org/wiki/Southernmost_point_buoy
Fort Zachary Taylor	$	601 Howard England Way	292-6713	https://www.floridastateparks.org/park/Fort-Taylor

Name	$	Address	Phone	Website
Key West Cemetary	F	701 Pauline St	292-8177	http://www.friendsofthekeywestcemetery.com
Mallory Square	F	400 Wall St	809-3700	https://www.mallorysquare.com
Mile Marker 0 for US1	F	490 Whitehead St	Just a Sign	https://en.wikipedia.org/wiki/U.S._Route_1
The Sandbox		1100 White St	896-5503	http://www.conchtv.com/key-west/the-sandbox-of-key-west
Margaritaville (the original)	$	500 Duval St	292-1435	http://www.margaritavillekeywest.com

Public Transportation

Name	Address	Phone	Website
Airport & Shuttle Transportation	PO Box 501439 Marathon, FL	289-999 7	http://www.keysshuttle.com
Key West Transit	5701 College Rd	809-391 0	http://www.keysshuttle.com
Dry Tortugas Ferry Service		866 575-506 8	https://www.drytortugasinfo.com/yankee-freedom-dry-tortugas-ferry/
Paradise Porters	100 Grinnell St	293-400 0	http://paradiseporters.com
Key West Express	100 Grinnell St	463-573 3	https://www.keywestexpress.net

Name	Address	Phone	Website
Key West International Airport	3491 S Roosevelt Blvd	809-5200	http://eyw.com
Seaplane Ferry		866 575-5068	https://www.drytortugasinfo.com/dry-tortugas-seaplane-excursion/

Web Cams

There are web cams located throughout Key West. The ones that I have below are the more popular. http://www.floridakeyswebcams.tv

Here are some of my favorites.

Location	Website
Hog's Breath Saloon	https://www.hogsbreath.com/keywest/index.php/hog-cam-bar-cam/
Mallory Square	https://www.mallorysquare.com/key-west-webcam/
Live Duval Street	http://www.liveduvalstreet.com
Southernmost Point	http://southernmostpointwebcam.com
Mile Marker 0	https://vacationhomesofkeywest.com/key-west-webcams.html

10 PERSONAL FAVORITES

Key West is not only a fun place to visit as a tropical paradise, many historical sites, and some great restaurants.

The trolley tours are a great way to not only reduce the amount of walking, but they also provide a fully narrated tour along the way. You have a couple of options depending on where you are staying. First, if you are staying at any of the resorts on the east side of town the Old Town Trolley would be your best bet. The City View and the Conch Train stay in the Historic District with more information on the historic area. All of the trolleys are fully narrated, and they all do a great job. Since I have driven for several touring companies, I am probably a little more critical. Our guide was John from Iowa/Pennsylvania, and he was great and both knowledgeable and entertaining. City View offered other discount coupons for attractions while riding the trolley.

There are plenty of things to do and not spend a lot of money. Here are some pictures of some of the free tourist attractions. One of the favorite spots is on "Sunset Pier" to watch the sunset. Both locals and tourist alike go for the evening viewing..

Sunset at Sunset Pier - Make sure you get there early...

It can get pretty crowded so make sure that you get there at least a half an hour before sunset.

The other two pictures are the Southernmost Point Buoy and the beginning of US 1 and mile marker 0.

Key West is loaded with lots and lots of water-related activities, in addition to museums and many free things that you can visit. Both pictures are just a short walk apart.

So after you get your picture at the buoy of the southernmost point. I guess I need to say that is correct for those of us that do not have access to the Coast Guard station. Actually, the real location is at the Coast Guard station. But I don't think that they have an icon quite like the one where you just had your photo at.

Can't go to Key West without a walk down Duvall Street for a drink, something to eat, or maybe some shopping.

The largest selection of souvenirs to take home is at the pier where the cruise ships come into Key West. This is the same area to pick up one of the city tours.

Fort Zachary Taylor is a beautiful and peaceful park on the west tip of Key West. It is also a place to see some amazing sunsets.

At the southern end of Duval Street after you pass an old fashion Denny's Diner will be Margaritaville on your right. They say it you might see Jimmy Buffet in Key West, but not with our luck. And of course we had to have a "Cheeseburger in Paradise" minus the fries and plus onion rings.

Cheeseburger in Paradise at Margaritaville

Here are some of my other favorites.

Location	Website
Hog's Breath Saloon	https://www.hogsbreath.com/keywest/index.php/hog-cam-bar-cam/
Mallory Square	https://www.mallorysquare.com/key-west-webcam/
Live Duval Street	http://www.liveduvalstreet.com
Southernmost Point	http://southernmostpointwebcam.com
Sloppy Joe's	https://sloppyjoes.com/cam-bar/

Location	Website
Mile Marker 0	https://vacationhomesofkeywest.com/key-west-webcams.html
Rum Barrel	http://www.mylivestreams.com/webcam/rum-barrel-live-streaming-bar-cam-key-west-florida/10539.html
Rick's and Dirty Harry's	http://ricksbarkeywest.com/pages/ricks-and-durty-harrys-cam

11 BISCAYNE OVERVIEW

Biscayne became a National Monument in 1968 and was enlarged and then became a National Park in 1980. The park covers approximately 173,000 acres, of which 95% is under water. It is located in southern Florida approximately 15 miles south of Miami, FL and was visited by 446,961 visitors in 2017. The Dante Fascell Visitor Center is located at the end of SW 328th Street, Homestead, Florida. From the Florida turnpike take exit 6 and turn south on SW 137 Avenue, then left on the SW 328th Street approximately 3 mile to the entrance to the park.

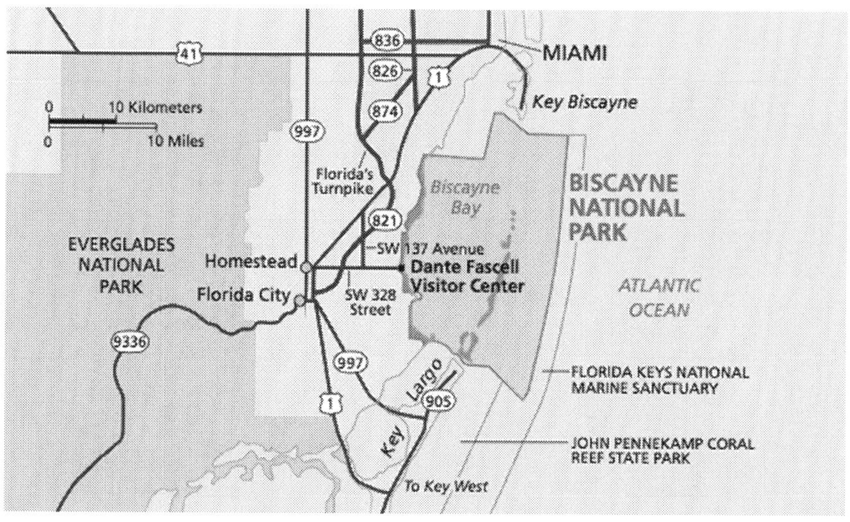

- **Contact Information:** 9700 SW 328th Street, Sir Lancelot Jones Way, Homestead, FL 33033
- **Website:** https://www.nps.gov/bisc/index.htm
- **Physical Address:** 9700 SW 328th Street, Sir Lancelot Jones Way, Homestead, FL 33033
- **Phone number:** (305) 230-1144
- **GPS Coordinates:** 25°27'50"N 80°20'06"W
- **ADA Accessibility:** The visitor center is accessible; however, the trails

are not recommended due to the terrain variations. The Island Boat Tour is ADA accessible.

- **Admission Fee:** FREE providing that you have a boat or a friend with a boat or you take the Island Tour boat ride to Boca Chita Key.

- **Hours:** Open every day, 24 hours a day. The Dante Fascell Visitor Center is open daily from 9 a.m. -5 p.m., closed Christmas Day. The Convoy Point area is open daily from 7 a.m. - 5:30 pm.

- **Pet Information:** Pets are not permitted on the Island Boat Tours.

- **Passport Stamp Location:** Dante Fascell Visitor Center Desk near the front desk.

Biscayne National Park total acreage consists mainly of water. There are 17 islands that are part of the 12 keys, which is located off of the southern coast of Florida, east of Homestead, FL between Key Biscayne and Key Largo.

Elliot, the largest Key, and Boca Chita Key are only areas where camping is permitted and accessible only by boat. Currently the only way to go camping on either key is by your privately owned boat or possibly chartering one to drop you off and pick you up, but I have heard that it would be very expensive and hard to find. Even with my searching I did not find one that advertises as a camping charter.

I do know that the NPS is looking to fill that void. So even if you don't own a boat don't give up just quite yet. Biscayne National Park is looking to offer that service hopefully in the near future. And like all of the parks, they will release the information through their Social Media such as Instagram, Twitter, and Facebook as soon as it is available. I will also post it on my Facebook page at: www.facebook.com/NationalParkPlanningGuides/.

12 BISCAYNE HISTORY

Early Beginnings

The park began approximately 100,000 years in the formation of the coral reef that extends down to the southern tip of Florida at Key West. The coral reef that we have today is a fragile eco system made up of billions of very small animals that live together to form the beautiful coral that we see today.

The Keys within the park boundaries have been home to Indians, early settlers, and the rich and famous.

It was citizens that in the early 1900's that wanted to protect the coral from being destroyed by growth and pollution, even though local and state government did not want to protect the area. A small group of citizens banded together and presented their case to the Federal Government. This led to the creation of the National Monument in 1968 and then the creations of Biscayne National Park in 1980.

Next to the lighthouse is a historic cannon that was believed to be used by Mr. Honeywell on the 4th of July when he would fire it off.

One of the millionaires that owned property included Mark C. Honeywell, owner of the Boca Chita Key. He built most of the structures on the island that can still be seen today. Those include the lighthouse, seaplane ramp, chapel, pavilion, large garage complex, and an arch bridge across the canal. His house was built out of wood and, even though it was destroyed by fire, you can still see the foundation on the island.

Mr. Honeywell built a 65 foot tall lighthouse as a navigation aid to reach his island. One small problem: he did not get permission to build the lighthouse from the United States Coast Guard, and since it was not on navigational charts, they would not allow him to operate it.

13 BISCAYNE ACTIVITIES

Hiking in the park

Boca Chita Key - There is a small trail approximately .5 miles that starts near the old sea plane ramp and goes around the island to the south and ends up on beach on the east side.

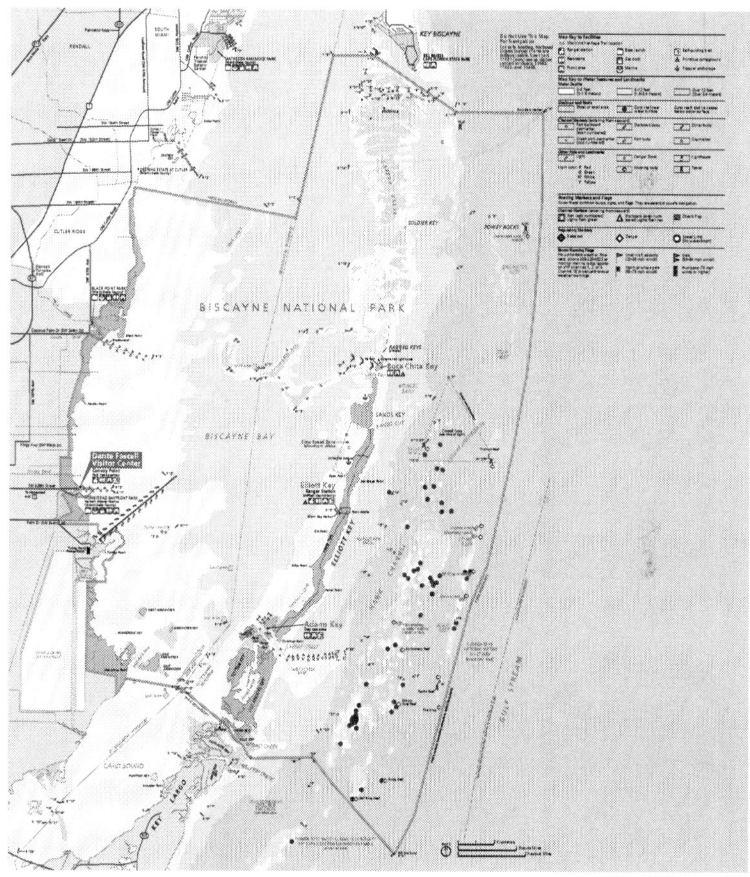

Elliott Key - Is the longest key that offers hiking, mainly north to south. There is a ranger station on the island, and this is the only island that has drinking water and showers.

Snorkeling and Scuba Diving

The park is like its sister park, the John Pennekamp Coral Reef State on it southern border, and offers excellent snorkeling and scuba diving, but remember not to touch the fragile coral eco system. Not only is the system fragile, but it is dangerous and can cause some nasty abrasions if you rub up against the coral, even by accident. Some things you may see include sponge, seagrass, elk horn coral, brain coral, angelfish, trumpet fish, parrotfish, and southern stingray. In the bay you may also see bottlenose dolphin.

NPS Activities and Programs

Here is the website for the calendar of events at Biscayne National Park: https://www.nps.gov/bisc/planyourvisit/calendar.htm.
Listed below were the programs offered in February when we went there:
*The programs do change so make sure that you connect to the website above to see what is going on when you plan your visit.

Guided Boat Tours - The boat tours are offered at 10 a.m. and 1 p.m. on select Thursdays, Fridays, Saturdays, and Sundays. It is a three hour guided tour by Biscayne National Park. As part of the tour you will be able to see the most northern key in the park, Boca Chita Key. In addition, on the island is a historic and iconic lighthouse. It is recommended to call the visitor center bookstore and reserve a seat by calling 786-335-3644. You will be riding on the Pelican Skipper, a 45 foot catamaran, that is ADA accessible.

I took the tour, and our tour guide Deborah did a great job. She had a lot of local history and pointed out animal life and birds along the journey. This is a very popular tour, so make sure that you call ahead to put your name on the list.

Earth, Air, Water - This program is FREE

Family Fun Fest - This program is FREE, 1 p.m. -4 p.m., and is usually offered only once a month, so be sure to look at the National Park calendar for availability

Park after Dark Programs - This program is FREE

ENCOUNTERS: Friend or Foe? - This program is FREE

14 BISCAYNE ACCOMMODATIONS

Camping in the park

Biscayne National Parks does not offer any camping on the mainland side of the park. And camping is permitted only on two of the islands (Boca Chita Key and Elliott Key), and mooring for boats is at Sands Key.

Boca Chita Key - There is a harbor for docking your boat, restrooms are nearby, and most of the original Honeywell structures are still in use today, except for his wooden house that was destroyed by a fire.

Elliot Key - Has a ranger station, harbor for docking your boat, fresh water, and restrooms and showers are nearby. They also off-shore for night moorings.

Local Hotels and Motels

Name	Address	Phone	Website
Courtyard by Marriott	2905 N E 9th St, Homestead, FL	(305) 257-4333	http://www.marriott.com/hotels/travel/miahs-courtyard-miami-homestead/?scid=bb1a189a-fec3-4d19-a255-54ba596febe2
Fairway Inn	100 SE 1st Ave, Florida City, FL	(305) 248-4202	http://www.fairwayinnfl.com
Hampton Inn & Suites	2855 N E 9th St, Homestead, FL	(305) 257-7000	http://hamptoninn3.hilton.com/en/hotels/florida/hampton-inn-and-suites-miami-south-homestead-HSTFLHX/index.html
Super 8 Florida City	1202 N Krome Ave, Florida City, FL	(305) 245-0311	https://www.wyndhamhotels.com/super-8/florida-city-florida/super-8-florida-city-homestead/overview?CID=LC:SE:20160927:Rio:Local

Name	Address	Phone	Website
Floridian Hotel	990 N Homestead Blvd, Homestead, FL	(305) 247-7020	http://floridianhotel.com
Hotel Redland	5 S Flagler Ave, Homestead, FL	(305) 246-1904	http://www.hotelredland.com
Travelodge Florida	409 SE 1st Ave, Florida City, FL	(305) 482-1961	https://www.wyndhamhotels.com/travelodge/florida-city-florida/travelodge-florida-city-homestead-everglades/overview?CID=LC:TL:20160927:Rio:Local&iata=00065402
Quality Inn	333 S.E. 1st Ave., US Hwy. #1, Florida City, FL	(786) 465-7600	https://www.choicehotels.com/florida/florida-city/quality-inn-hotels/fl432?source=gyxt
TownPlace Suites by Marriott	935 NE 30th Ave, Homestead, FL	(305) 248-2001	http://www.marriott.com/hotels/travel/miatm-towneplace-suites-miami-homestead/?scid=bb1a189a-fec3-4d19-a255-54ba596febe2
Best Western	411 S Krome Ave, Florida City, FL	(305) 246-5100	https://www.bestwestern.com/en_US/book/hotel-details.10254.html?iata=00171880&ssob=BLBWI0004G&cid=BLBWI0004G:google:gmb:10254
Ramada Florida City	124 E Palm Dr, Florida City, FL	(305) 230-2322	https://www.wyndhamhotels.com/ramada/florida-city-florida/ramada-florida-city/overview?CID=LC:RA:20160927:RIO:Local:SM-rasatl

Name	Address	Phone	Website
Home2 Suites by Hilton	77 NE 3rd St, Florida City, FL	(305) 248-3155	http://home2suites3.hilton.com/en/hotels/florida/home2-suites-by-hilton-florida-city-fl-MIAFAHT/index.html
Holiday Inn Express	35200 S Dixie Hwy, Florida City, FL	(305) 247-3414	https://www.ihg.com/holidayinnexpress/hotels/us/en/florida-city/fcffl/hoteldetail?cm_mmc=GoogleMaps-_-EX-_-USA-_-FCFFL

Local Campgrounds

Name	Address	Phone	Website
Boardwalk RV Resort	100 NE 6th Avenue, Homestead, FL	(305) 248-2487	http://boardwalkrv.com
Florida City Camp Site and RV Park	601 NW 3rd Ave, Homestead, FL	(305) 248-7889	
Flamingo Campground T Loop		(239) 695-0124	
Southern Comfort RV Resort	345 Palm Dr, Florida City, FL	(305) 248-6909	https://www.socorv.com
Long Pine Key Campground	Entrance to Everglades NP	(305) 242-7873	https://www.nps.gov/ever/planyourvisit/longpinecamp.htm
Goldcoaster RV Resort	34850 SW 187th Ave, Homestead, FL	(888) 833-3929	https://www.sunrvresorts.com/Community/GLD
Miami Everglades RV Resort	20675 SW 162nd Ave, Miami, FL	(305) 233-5300	http://www.rvonthego.com/florida/miami-everglades-rv-resort/
Pelican Cay RV Park	299 Morris Ave, Key Largo, FL	(305) 451-5223	http://pelicancayharbor.com

15 NPS LOCATIONS NEARBY

	Website
Everglades National Park	https://home.nps.gov/ever/index.htm
Big Cypress National Preserve	https://home.nps.gov/bicy/index.htm

ISBN-10: - 1-946490-16-4

ISBN-13: - 978-1-946490-16-2

Notes

Notes

Notes

Notes

Made in the USA
Columbia, SC
12 December 2023

28306439R00037